Original title:
The Key Around Your Neck

Copyright © 2025 Creative Arts Management OÜ
All rights reserved.

Author: Nathaniel Blackwood
ISBN HARDBACK: 978-1-80586-147-8
ISBN PAPERBACK: 978-1-80586-619-0

Guardian of Hidden Truths

A trinket dangled, swaying slow,
Who knew it held secrets, in its glow?
It jangles with laughter, a tune so bright,
Do you dance or do you run? It's quite a sight!

On a quest for wisdom, I tripped on a cat,
The truth slipped out from beneath its hat.
Each giggle echoes, a riddle in play,
Who knew such fun could brighten the day?

Talisman of Secrets Untold

Around my neck, what's this charm?
A wizard's hiccup? A frog's alarm?
Twisting and turning, what could it be?
A spell on my sandwich? Or a dance with a bee?

Twirling at parties, my necklace does spin,
Revealing my antics, where do I begin?
It whispers confessions, under the moon,
While I juggle my chores, a comedic cartoon!

Token of Celestial Encounters

A bauble of sorts, from outer space,
With every bounce, it has its own grace.
Aliens giggle, I swear I heard,
Laughing at me like a jester absurd!

In the cosmos' cradle, we play hide and seek,
With intergalactic friends, I'm feeling quite meek.
They tap dance on stars, sharing laughter and dreams,
While I trip on stardust, it's not what it seems!

Essence of Unseen Realms

Here's a charm that touts the unknown,
A giggle from goblins, it's modestly grown.
Riddles on raindrops, floated on air,
It teases with whispers, beyond compare!

With sprites and fairies, the fun never ends,
Around my neck, it spins and transcends.
Each chuckle a portal, to worlds so bizarre,
I chase shadows of humor, it's my own memoir!

Whispered Unlocking

In a pocket, a secret resides,
Waiting for laughter to be the guides.
A twist and a turn, what do you hear?
Just giggles and hiccups, never a fear.

With every chime, the nonsense flows,
Jokes in the air, where mischief grows.
Unlock the silly, let worries flee,
For laughter is best when it's wild and free.

Heart's Hidden Locket

Around the neck, a charm so quaint,
Whispers of silliness, it loves to paint.
Each bounce and jingle is a secret shared,
In this merry world, none are scared.

Crafty little tales hide in its gold,
Of clowns and cookies, all lovingly told.
With each flip, a giggle, a toast,
This pendant of joy, it matters the most.

Chain of Possibilities

A chain so bright, it dances in light,
Linking up dreams in playful delight.
With a jiggle and jig, the world seems right,
Turn the lock, let the fun take flight.

Comedic gems lie in each little clasp,
Of misfit adventures, a quirky gasp.
Unlock the riddle, let joy take a peek,
In this chain, the future's never bleak.

Necklace of Forgotten Doors

This trinket holds tales from long ago,
Keys to the laughter, they start to flow.
With a twist and a tease, the doors swing wide,
A goofy parade coming forth with pride.

Each door that opens reveals a jest,
Happiness waiting, an endless quest.
So wear it with glee, let your heart be free,
Unlock the whimsy, just wait and see!

Worn Wonders

A pendant dangles, wild and free,
Tales of mishaps, just like me.
It clinks and clatters, quite a sound,
In pockets deep, lost treasures found.

It once opened locks, oh what a thrill,
Now it just jangles, it's lost its skill.
With each funny jolt, I can't help but grin,
My trusty charm holds history within.

Gateway to the Soul

An odd little trinket, shaped like a star,
Claimed it unlocks dreams from afar.
But every night, it's a fierce debate,
As to whether it's magic or just fate.

I'd worn it once, thinking it wise,
But it just led to awkward goodbyes.
A gateway it seems, to comic relief,
Bringing smiles where there should be grief.

Medallion of Mysteries

A shiny bauble, hiding secrets galore,
It jingles and jangles, oh what a chore!
Claimed to reveal what the heart did hide,
But really just shows who's clumsy inside.

This medallion of chuckles, wrapped in a jest,
Promised adventures, gave me the rest.
Each knock and each scrape, a legend in hand,
As I trip over tales, life's funny and grand.

Emblem of Doors Yet Unlocked

An emblem I wear, both proud and loud,
Each door it should open, yet I'm left wowed.
With twists and with turns, it leads me astray,
Unlocking the laughter in my clumsy way.

It's seen better days, with scratches to show,
Stuck in the metal, the stories do flow.
An emblem of blunders, through laughter's door,
Unlocking the joy that I simply adore.

Medallion of Dreams Yet to Come

In pockets deep, a treasure hides,
A shiny charm where laughter bides.
It jingles softly with every move,
A dance of hopes that makes us groove.

Upon my chest, it swings and sways,
Reminding me of silly days.
When wishes wore a playful grin,
And I believed I'd always win.

Chain of Unwritten Legends

A tangled twist of stories bright,
Each link a giggle, pure delight.
It drags behind, with a comical clink,
And in its shadow, I stop to think.

Of heroes bold with floppy feet,
On couches grand where snacks we eat.
Where battles fought in games of chance,
And every loss leads to a dance!

Token of Lost Tomorrows

I wear a badge from yesteryear,
A memento of mischief, it's clear.
It grins at fate with a cheeky wink,
As if to say, 'Let's never think!'

For every flop, it shines with pride,
A story wrapped in dreamy tide.
We chase the sunsets, share a laugh,
And squeeze the juice from life's own gaffe.

Pendant of Fleeting Moments

Hanging low, like a pendulum's swing,
Whispers of chaos, let joy take wing.
It laughs at time, a mischievous prank,
Reminding me to dance, not blank!

In fleeting frames, we spin in cheer,
With every tick, bring laughter near.
So round we go, in a merry whirl,
Embracing our dreams, my silly pearl.

Guardian of Secrets

A box of secrets, locked so tight,
The guardian giggles, what a sight!
Whispers and chuckles, a tricky tease,
Every twist and turn, just to appease.

Hidden behind a smile so sly,
Questions arise, do they lie?
With every secret, there's laughter anew,
You ask for the truth, but who has a clue?

Emblem of the Unknown

A badge of honor, or a quirky mess,
Who needs answers? It's all just a guess!
Wearing it proudly, with flair and style,
Unlocking mischief, go on, stay awhile.

What lies beyond? A riddle awaits,
The more you ponder, the more it elates.
A symbol of chaos, and a little fun,
Who knew such nonsense could weigh a ton?

A Path in Plain Sight

Right under our noses, the clues do lie,
A silly dance will help you fly!
With a hop and a skip, it's no parade,
But follow the giggles, don't be dismayed.

A treasure hunt wrapped in a grin,
You search for answers, not sure you'll win.
The path is wild, with bumps and laughs,
Lost in the journey, let's scribble our drafts.

Accessing the Unseen

A secret door painted bright blue,
What's behind it? A llama that flew!
Through giggles and grins, and riddles galore,
Step through the curtain, let's explore more.

The visions are wacky, the fun is immense,
Caution advised or just common sense?
What's hidden in laughter, let's take a peek,
Access the unseen with a chuckle or squeak!

Whispering Chains of Fate

In pockets of laughter, secrets reside,
A jingle of fortune, where dreams often hide.
Clumsy adventures, oh, what a sight,
Every turn taken, a new twist of light.

With each little bump, tales come to play,
For every misstep, there's joy on the way.
A charm that can giggle when lost in a rush,
Dancing through mishaps, it adds to the crush.

Twisting and turning, like some wild dance,
With whispers of fate, we seize every chance.
In a world of blunders, it's laughter we seek,
The happiest treasures are found at their peak.

So come join the quirk, let's look for the glee,
In the chains of our fate, we'll find jubilee.
For every wrong turn, a chuckle is made,
With a twist of good fortune, let joy fill the shade.

Amulet of Inner Journeys

With a wink and a nudge, we venture inside,
An amulet's glow, our laughter as guide.
Each whimsy ignites, the more we explore,
To inner realms where silliness soars.

A giggle allured by a spark of delight,
Suddenly tripping on clouds made of light.
In tunnels of thought, we don our best grin,
Every twist and tangle, a chance to begin.

Oh, the quest through our minds brings whimsical cheer,
With wonders around, it's fun we hold dear.
A cape made of chuckles and thoughts that are bright,
We journey together, into the delight.

So let's toast to the journeys that make us all grin,
With laughter in pockets, let the fun all begin.
From amulet roads, to halls made of dreams,
In every small twist, there's joy in the seams.

Jewel of Hidden Passages

A jewel glimmers bright, with secrets galore,
In hidey-holes laughing behind every door.
With whispers of mischief, it opens the fun,
Each passage discovered, new chuckles begun.

Recesses of laughter, where silliness sings,
A treasure to find in the flapping of wings.
Where doodles of joy scribble tales on the wall,
In winding adventures, we laugh through it all.

With sparkles of humor tucked away in the groove,
Every turn in the maze, cheers up the move.
In the depths of our hearts, it's treasures we keep,
A jewel of the moments that make the heart leap.

So gather your giggles, let them shine bright,
For in playful escapes, we chase pure delight.
Through hidden passages, let laughter unfold,
In the shine of the jewel, our stories are told.

Necklace of Resilient Hearts

A necklace of joy, brightly sewn with our dreams,
In moments of laughter, hope gleams and redeems.
With each twist and turn, and a wink from the sun,
This dance of resilience has only begun.

A pop and a fizz, the playful sparks fly,
With hearts made of giggles stretching far to the sky.
Through trials and troubles, we chuckle and cheer,
For the strength in our laughter, it's crystal clear.

With beads of affection and charms that inspire,
This necklace we wear sets our spirits afire.
Each knot, an adventure, rich stories to share,
Through the laughter and smiles, we rise from despair.

So shine like a jewel, let the fun never part,
In the necklace of life, we find resilient hearts.
For what we put forth in giggles and glee,
Is the magic that binds our hearts, truly free.

Key to the Forgotten

In a pocket, lost it lay,
Dusty memories gone astray.
Now it jingles, can't ignore,
What was it for? I'm not so sure.

Mice now nest where dreams had bloomed,
Unlocking laughs in rooms entombed.
A relic of some life I led,
Where doorways whispered, 'Come, be fed!'

Emblem of Inner Strength

A trinket bold, a tiny charm,
Or is it just a good luck alarm?
"It opens doors!" I proudly said,
But it's really just a bottle for bread.

With each new jiggle, I feel so grand,
My aching back can barely stand.
But hey, if I can laugh a bit,
I'll keep this bangler—oh, it's a hit!

Locket of Passing Moments

Inside this case, a face appeared,
Not mine, but I can't say I jeered.
What fun it is to wonder why,
My past is such a quirky guy!

In family portraits, we all convene,
A cousin's hair could turn to green.
Each snapshot sealed in a graceful clasp,
I pull it out, then start to gasp!

Adventure's Silent Pendant

On this chain, a whistle dangles,
I thought for birds, it strangely wrangles.
But every time I give a blow,
The cat just stares; it's quite the show!

Chasing dreams and squeaky sounds,
I'm off to where absurdity abounds.
Each clink and clank, my merry tune,
An anthem sung to silly afternoons!

Locket of Soul's Whispers

In a tiny locket, secrets hide,
With whispers of my soul inside.
When I bend down to tie my shoe,
It giggles softly, just like you.

A heartbeat's echo trapped in gold,
It tells me jokes, so brave, so bold.
"Why did the bird not cross the street?"
"To avoid the cat with sneaky feet!"

Jangling gently, it spins around,
Like a merry-go-round that knows no bounds.
When strangers ask what it can do,
I wink and say, "It sings for you!"

A touch of magic, a sprinkle of cheer,
With every chuckle, my charm's quite near.
So if you're ever feeling down,
Just grab my locket, wear that crown!

Chain of Resonant Paths

On my neck hangs a curious chain,
It clinks and clanks, but gives no pain.
"Where does it lead?" the followers ask,
"Is it a mystery, or just a task?"

"It's a shortcut to joys!" I gleefully say,
"To ice cream shops and games all day!"
It twists and turns like a winding road,
But leads to fun, as the stories flowed.

With every step, it sings a tune,
Of lost sock gnomes by the light of the moon.
"Why do they dance on laundry days?"
"Because they love all the cotton rays!"

So follow this chain, my feet will glide,
Through laugh-filled places, come take a ride!
For every jingle is a happy sound,
Let's uncover the joy that's all around!

Token of Wizard's Secrets

A shiny token hangs from my chest,
Claiming to capture the wizard's best.
"What's inside?" they ask with glee,
"Chocolate frogs or a duck in a tree?"

"Neither, my friend, it's full of fun!
It boasts a spell to make you run!
When life gets heavy, give it a shake,
And create giggles for everyone's sake!"

A fellow wizard passed it along,
Said magic thrives where laughter's strong.
So I wear it proudly, it twinkles bright,
Unlocking smiles day and night!

"What's the secret?" they plead in awe,
I grin and twirl my charm with a draw.
"A recipe for joy, easy to brew,
Just mix in a dance, and shout 'Whoo-hoo!'"

Pendant of Life's Multi-Paths

A pendant glimmers, bright and bold,
Claiming to guide hearts young and old.
"Which way to go?" travelers ask me,
I chuckle and point, "All roads lead to glee!"

When choices loom and paths collide,
This pendant chirps with laughter inside.
"Take a left, take a right, it matters not,
Every journey is a treasure trove, a thought!"

"Why's it so shiny?" they blink in surprise,
"Is it magic or just clever lies?"
"Both!" I reply, "And here's the key,
It giggles in moments of jubilee!"

So wear it close, let laughter ensue,
For life is a dance, and joy will ensue.
This pendant knows every twist and bend,
Calling your heart to find a friend!

Talisman of Untold Stories

In pockets deep, a trinket glows,
With secrets held, nobody knows.
It jangles loud with every move,
A comic dance, just watch it groove.

A lock it finds, absurd but neat,
To open laughter, what a treat!
Yet in my grasp, it stays in place,
It mocks my stillness, such a grace.

A fabled tale that can't be told,
Of silly heroes, brave and bold.
I chase the tales, like chased my cat,
But still it binds, where's this thing at?

With every jingle, giggles rise,
A magic charm, oh what a prize!
It keeps me laughing, so alive,
This talisman, I shall not hide.

Orb of Hushed Echoes

A round little orb, shine bright and round,
Whispers secrets without a sound.
In quiet corners, it starts to sing,
Of silly things that make hearts swing.

It holds the breeze of forgotten dreams,
A treasure where humor beams.
I tickle it, it chuckles back,
In giggly fits, it starts to crack.

An awkward glow in monotone,
Cracks me up when I'm alone.
It throws me tales of wobbly chairs,
And goofy dances in mismatched pairs.

With every spark, it brightens the room,
Spreading joy like an endless bloom.
It hides in shadows, loves to tease,
This orb of laughs, oh what a breeze!

Key to the Infinite

A wiggly thing, shaped like a fork,
Unlocks the gates of wacky quirk.
In my pocket, it jingles and shakes,
A silly tool for all my mistakes.

It opens doors to places unknown,
Where sock monsters might have grown.
I twist and turn, it fits just right,
And bursts with laughter, sheer delight!

Yet when I grasp it, poof! It's gone,
Into thin air, like a fleeting dawn.
It giggles softly, playing hide,
This key to nonsense, as my guide.

With a tickle here, a jiggle there,
It leads me to places full of flair.
For every blunder, it holds the spell,
This key to fun, it rings so well!

Locket of Hidden Light

A locket swings, a charming beast,
Hiding laughter, oh what a feast.
With every click, a funny sound,
It's full of giggles, joy unbound.

It hides away some quirky sparks,
From silly ducks to dancing larks.
With each embrace, it starts to glow,
Unleashing chuckles, a bright show.

In corners dark, the secrets lie,
Of whoopee cushions and cake gone by.
A treasure chest of jest and glee,
Unlock the fun, come dance with me!

So wear it close, this gleaming charm,
With every heartbeat, spread the balm.
For hidden light brings giggles free,
In every moment, let laughter be!

Gateway to the Unseen

In a world where socks go missing,
I found a door, all shiny and glistening.
I gave it a jangle, made a funny face,
And in I stumbled, into outer space.

The cat was waiting, with a hat and a grin,
He offered me coffee, and a cheerful spin.
We danced on the stars, in mismatched shoes,
What a sight to see, in such cosmic blues!

A keyhole appeared, I squinted and peered,
The whispers of donuts, I swiftly endared.
With sprinkles and laughter in every bite,
We feasted 'til dawn, on pure delight!

When morning arrived, I blinked at the sun,
Was it all just a dream? Oh, what fun!
I skipped past the door and laughed as I played,
In a world without keys, under sun-soaked parade.

Charm of Hidden Pathways

Through a hedge with a wink, I stumbled quite wide,
Found paths with their secrets, trying to hide.
With lanterns of jellybeans lighting the way,
I giggled at squirrels, at their nutty display.

I took a short turn, met a frog on a throne,
He offered me snacks and a fine ice cream cone.
We chatted of fables, and summer rain,
He croaked out a tune, like a jazzy refrain.

We hopped to a garden, where flowers wore shoes,
With dancing daffodils, and theatrical blues.
Each bloom had a story, so silly and bright,
Beneath their odd petals, burst pure delight!

As twilight approached, I watched them all sway,
In a whimsical waltz, at the close of the day.
With laughter and joy, I waved them adieu,
What a charming adventure, with my colorful crew!

Necklace of Unspoken Truths

In a box of odd trinkets, I found a rare charm,
It sparkled with shadows and a hint of alarm.
I held it up high, just a tad unsure,
And then out popped a parrot, with a joke to explore!

He squawked of a pirate, who couldn't find loot,
Said the treasure was laughter, in a rubbery suit.
We burst into giggles, a comical sight,
While searching for jewels in the dark of the night.

With each little truth, like a bobblehead dance,
We shared secret giggles, and the wildest romance.
I wore this fine necklace, with tales so absurd,
For every new laugh was the best hidden word!

In the end, we found, truth's not what it seems,
It's wrapped up in laughter and whimsical dreams.
With a wink and a smile, I tucked it away,
For my heart's the treasure, come what may!

Harbinger of New Horizons

A paperclip wizard on the edge of my desk,
Conjured up portals, quite quirky and fresh.
With a twist and a twirl, he unveiled a spree,
Of journeys to places that were wiggly free.

We bopped through the cosmos, with upside-down charts,
Rode rainbow-tongued unicorns, melting our hearts.
We shared jellybean wishes and mango-flavored stars,
While playing hide and seek with these meteoric cars!

A bubble of joy, we floated right high,
Laughed at the comets that whizzed by the sky.
Each giggle a beacon, each chuckle a guide,
On this wild adventure, together we glide.

When we landed back home, with a pop and a fun,
I thanked my dear wizard for the joy we'd begun.
With magic like this, oh what a delight,
To chase all our dreams, on a whimsy-filled night!

Spirit of the Unrevealed

In a land where secrets hide,
A squirrel wears a crown of pride.
It chases dreams on tiny feet,
Twirling in a dance, oh what a treat!

A cat with glasses, wise yet sly,
Sips tea while watching clouds go by.
With laughter ringing in the air,
Wonders bubble without a care.

In every nook, a tale unfolds,
With bubbles of joy, the magic molds.
A funny hat finds its new home,
As giggles echo and spirits roam.

The Magic in Misfits

A penguin skates on frozen dreams,
Frantically juggling creamy creams.
With a wink and a slide, all is fun,
Chasing a rhino under the sun!

A giraffe bids a fond goodnight,
In pajamas, oh what a sight!
Bananas dance in the moonlight glow,
While ticklish whispers begin to flow.

In silly socks that don't quite match,
Misfits gather for a crazy batch.
With hearts so light and spirits high,
Their laughter rings against the sky.

Necklace of Intentions

A cat with a crayon draws the map,
Where unicorns play and don't take a nap.
With ribbons and bows, they twist and twine,
Chasing the stars, oh how they shine!

A dog in a tutu does a ballet,
Twisting and turning, come join the fray!
Singing a song with a humorous twist,
As the moon laughs too, you can't miss!

With friends all around in vibrant hues,
They craft a world of sparkly views.
In this realm where silliness reigns,
Even the clouds wear silly chains.

Portal of Possibility

A marshmallow dragon gives a toast,
To all the folks who love to boast.
Flip-flops anoint the great parade,
In a festival where dreams are made!

A rabbit with sneakers hops along,
Telling stories, oh so strong!
With carrots dressed in party attire,
They dance like flames, bright and higher.

Through the portal, a world unfolds,
With laughter and wonder, oh so bold.
Here mismatched socks lead the way,
To a comedy show where puns don't sway!

Amulet of Lost Opportunities

A shiny trinket dangles low,
With tales of where I shouldn't go.
Its glimmer tricks, my hopes it stirs,
Oh look! Another chance, I slur!

I wear it proudly, what a cheek,
The road not taken, oh so bleak.
Each clink and clatter brings delight,
Reminds me of my frightful flight!

A missed party, a skipped date too,
This charm just laughs at what I screw.
In every blunder, it gives a wink,
Encouraging me to overthink!

Oh silly amulet, what a jest,
Embracing all my very best.
With every giggle and each glance,
I strut around as fate's own dance!

Pendant of Unraveled Mysteries

This pendant swings with secrets bold,
With riddles wrapped in silver and gold.
A mystery, it beams with glee,
While I just scratch my puzzling knee!

It whispers tales of socks gone missing,
Of lost cat toys that used to glisten.
Wrapped in laughter, none seem clear,
But hey, I guess that's part of the cheer!

With every jingle, it's quite a show,
Unraveling chaos, oh how it flows!
It chuckles softly, 'Find the clue!'
But I just giggle—what can I do?

Oh pendant dear, don't hide away,
Just dangle low, and let me play.
Mysteries wrapped in comedic grace,
I wear your charm with a silly face!

Medallion of Fate's Embrace

Oh this medallion, heavy and round,
With a fate that tumbles all around.
It pulls my heart, or is it my shoe?
Who knows what this shiny piece will do?

It teeters lightly on my chest,
Promising luck—at least a jest.
With every shimmy and silly jig,
I wonder if fate's just a big rig!

Whispers of fortune, or is it jest?
Each step I take, my doubts are blessed.
As I trip, it chuckles, "Oops, too late!"
With every tumble, I find my fate!

Medallion buddy, hold me tight,
For I'm diving into this goofy flight.
Embrace my blunders, make me grin,
Together we'll waddle, let the fun begin!

Dangles of Destiny

These dangles swing, a playful sight,
With every wiggle, they take flight.
Destiny giggles, a whimsical cheer,
While I just grumble, 'Oh dear, oh dear!'

They dangle low, oh what a tease,
Promising wonders, a laugh at ease.
Every slip, a chance for joy,
In mishaps, find the little boy!

Slapstick moments, oh aren't they grand?
Destiny winks, a guiding hand.
With each little tug, I'm taken away,
Laughing loudly at myself today!

Oh dangles dear, let's prance along,
In this comedy, you can't go wrong.
With a dash of luck and a sprinkle of fun,
Together we'll shine, dance, and run!

Whispering Talismans

In the pocket, a secret chat,
Favors from a friendly cat.
Whispers float on a chilly breeze,
Unlocking wonders, if you please.

Jingle, jangle, let's all dance,
Finding treasures with a glance.
Each step bursts with silly giggles,
Watch out for those silly wiggles.

Behind a door, a joke awaits,
Knock and dive into the fates.
With laughter echoing through the hall,
Each moment's magic, after all.

So swing that charm and make a wish,
Life's a joke, it's quite delish.
The world's a stage, let's play our part,
With gleeful tales that warm the heart.

Medallion of New Beginnings

Upon my chest, a shiny thing,
Bubbling hopes like they can sing.
Each morning's dance, a new debut,
Bumps and hiccups did ensue.

Twirl around like a dizzy bee,
Who knew life could be so free?
Each mishap, it waves and grins,
With sparkly tales where laughter spins.

Just flip the charm like flipping pancakes,
Syrupy fun, that's what it makes.
Sass it up with every twist,
In life's grand dance, you can't resist.

So wear your medallion with delight,
Jump through clouds, take flight tonight.
In every stumble, find a cheer,
New beginnings give a hearty leer.

Jewel of Untold Adventures

Hidden gems spark in the light,
Each glimmer yells, 'What a sight!'
Get ready for mischief, my friend,
Journeys start with giggles to lend.

Pack your suitcase, don't forget snacks,
Get your map and avoid the cracks.
Each corner hides a tale to tell,
Unexpected twists cast a spell.

Skip on bricks that jiggle and rock,
Every stumble? Just tick-tock!
With a jewel glittering on your chest,
We'll paint the world and laugh the best.

So let's be bold and seek the strange,
In every odd step, there's a change.
Life's a treasure chest, just wait and see,
The adventures are as funny as can be.

Unlocking Life's Eclipses

Behind a door, shadows poke,
In the light, we share a joke.
Eclipses hide but show to play,
Twisted paths lead us astray.

Open wide with a grin so wide,
Chase the ducks, join the ride.
In every mishap, here's a twist,
What's more funny than life's list?

Each knock reveals a silly clue,
With laughter spilling like morning dew.
Unlock the giggles lurking near,
In the dark, find cheer, my dear.

So embrace the quirks, laugh out loud,
We dance between the silly crowd.
With life's eclipses, don't you fret,
Each twist's a story we won't forget.

Amulet of Life's Secrets

In the pocket of whimsy, I keep a charm,
Jingles and jangles, it does no harm.
With each little twist, it brings such delight,
Unlocking the laughter that dances at night.

It whispers of mischief, oh what a tease,
Promises fortunes with just a breeze.
A magic trick here, a joke there too,
In this tiny trinket, fun breaks through!

Dancing around like a puppy in spring,
I thought it a lure, but it's just a fling.
The world's secrets giggle, and chatter in rhyme,
This amulet's purpose? To waste some time!

So if you see me, with a grin so wide,
Know it's just my secret, I'll wear with pride.
Each giggle a door, each chuckle a gate,
In this silly mystery, I sit and await!

Precious Links of Time

Tick-tock, tick-tock, they dangle and sway,
Bright little circles that lead me astray.
One says it's lunchtime, another says 'dance,'
With these precious links, my day takes a chance.

They giggle in chaos, they wobble and roll,
Each twists and turns with a wink at my soul.
I ask where to go, they whisper and tease,
"Oh let's take a shortcut, let's shimmy with ease!"

Sometimes I ponder if they twist fate,
With a chuckle so deep, they simply create.
I might end up lost, wrapped around some whim,
But the laughter that follows makes every trip grim!

So here's to the moments, the fun and the ticking,
With links of pure joy that keep my heart kicking.
In this zany parade, I twirl and I spin,
With our wacky adventures, let the fun begin!

Heart's Cryptic Accessory

Around my neck hangs a puzzling charm,
It spins and it twirls, oh what a calm!
A heart that's encrypted, with giggles concealed,\nUnlocking the laughter, joy is revealed.

Each riddle it offers just makes me grin,
"Where's my left shoe?"; "Why isn't that pin?"
With every silly question it does propose,
I stumble through life like a clumsy rose.

A whimsical jester in disguise it seems,
Twirling my woes into fantastic dreams.
It leads me in circles, what a cheeky play,
Bouncing on smiles throughout the whole day!

So I wear it with glee, this merry delight,
My heart's funny accessory shines so bright.
Each giggle a secret, each laugh a clue,
With this cryptic gem, I'll dance life anew!

Symbol of Uncharted Paths

A quirky trinket held close to my chest,
Guides me to places where nonsense is best.
Each twist of its shine, a path to explore,
Unfolding adventures, oh, who could ask for more?

It chuckles and shimmies, with gates left ajar,
Leading me onward to a carnival star.
Lost in its whimsy, I wander and roam,
Finding new routes that somehow feel like home.

As it dances on threads of both laughter and fate,
I follow its whims, what an odd little mate!
With valleys of giggles and mountains of cheer,
This symbol of chaos draws me ever near.

So here I am, with a skip and a hop,
Searching for joy, never wanting to stop.
In this world full of laughter, I relish each laugh,
With my magical charm, I'm never out of half!

Enigma in Silver

A shiny trinket dangles free,
It bounces with a spirit, oh so glee.
A riddle wrapped in metal, it shines,
Unlocks the laughter, in playful designs.

It's not a treasure, nor a magic spell,
Just a quirky charm from a yard sale.
In a world so serious, it brings delight,
A curious oddity on a summer night.

With silly thoughts, it turns and twirls,
As if it holds the dreams of girls.
Each jingle brings a giggle, a cheer,
Messy hair and ice cream, no need to fear.

So wear it proudly, let your joy reflect,
In this playful enigma, we all connect.

The Token of Tomorrow

In the pocket of fate, a smile awaits,
Twirling secrets like those of old mates.
A little bobble, a whimsy of chance,
Hints of adventures, where we dance.

This tiny bauble may look quite dull,
But it promises mischief, oh so full.
With each jiggle, a giggle grows,
Who knows what tomorrow may expose?

It's not just metal; it holds a jest,
Of silly dreams, it knows the best.
A ticket to chaos, merely a chance,
To leap into fun with a merry prance.

So let it dangle, let it sway,
Encouraging whimsy in a playful way.
In this token, we find our cheer,
Tomorrow's laughter, always near.

Pendant of Dreams

A charm that jangles between my chest,
Woven with giggles, it's simply the best.
Oh, what a sight, it twinkles with glee,
Like the watchers of sunsets, just wait and see.

In dreams, it painted a world so bright,
With candy-colored skies and endless flights.
Each swing and sway, a flick of delight,
Tickling my heart with its fool's insight.

It's a silly reminder of laughter to pour,
Of rainy-day puddles and ice cream galore.
A tiny token of joy I wear,
Whispering secrets of silliness rare.

So join the dance, let your worries dissolve,
With this merry pendant, let's all evolve.
In a spark of absurdity, we'll all gleam,
Chasing the magic in a fleeting dream.

Keyed to the Uncharted

A little loop of whimsy on a string,
Whispers of places where giggles spring.
It's not a way in, but a joyful twirl,
Unlocking laughter in a playful whirl.

Every jingle tells a tale of cheer,
Of silly mischief that draws us near.
With no map in hand, we bravely embark,
Exploring the night in a friendly park.

A potion of chaos, a riddle in jest,
It holds all the secrets for a wild fest.
With each little collision, a chuckle ignites,
Adventures await under starry nights.

So don this marvel, let the fun commence,
In a world of laughter, let's lose all sense.
For a key made of giggles will surely reveal,
The sweetest adventures that make us feel.

Silhouette of Freedom

In the pocket of my jeans, a mystery lies,
A jangling noise, oh what a surprise!
Is it change or a relic, a secret surprise?
All my friends laugh, they roll their eyes.

With every jump, it jangles and sways,
My personal maraca for spontaneous plays!
I dance like a fool, in the sun's warm rays,
Freedom's anthem, in silly displays.

A rubber band snapped, and oh what a sight!
The pouch bursts open, I'm filled with delight.
A launch of old gum, and scrunchies take flight,
With this comical chaos, my heart feels so light.

In this playful journey of pockets and fun,
Who needs a map when you're under the sun?
Each clink and each clatter, a dash of a pun,
In the silhouette of laughter, I'm never outrun.

Locket of Longing

A locket that swings from my sweatshirt seam,
A tiny keepsake, or so it would seem.
What treasures it holds? I start to dream,
Maybe a sandwich, or fluff from a cream.

I open it wide with a dramatic flair,
Inside, it's just crumbs from my last snack affair.
I close it back up, with exaggerated care,
A real sentimental, low-caloric layer!

Is it a sign? Should I start saving more?
For treasures of snacks, or trinkets galore?
Each morsel reminds me, it's worth to explore,
This jewelry's just holding my lunch from the store.

So I wear it with pride, this locket so neat,
A charming oddity, a culinary feat.
My friends giggle softly, they can't take the heat,
But who knew that longing could taste oh so sweet?

Tethered Dreams

A ribbon of hopes tied tightly to me,
With bounce and with laughter, it's crafty and free.
Each tug and each pull is my destiny's key,
I skip to the rhythm, oh woe is the glee!

On winding paths, my tether can snag,
A tree, a stray dog, or my backpack's rag.
In moments of chaos, it starts to drag,
But I'm still the captain, no need to brag!

In the park, I trip, and I fall on my nose,
The dreams laugh out loud as the laughter just flows.
With every new tumble, my confidence grows,
A tethered adventurer, where silliness glows.

With each clumsiness, I'm grounded in fun,
Just tether my heart, and let dreams run.
In this wild world, I've already won,
With giggles and wiggles, my journey's begun.

Threads of Destiny

A ball of yarn, tangled up in my plan,
With colors so bright, it tugs and it ran.
I weave my own fate, like a silly old man,
With threads of absurdity, I craft what I can.

I try to knit wisdom, but it's all gone awry,
A scarf for a chicken, I giggle and sigh.
Each loop and each twist, it's a comical tie,
I'm dressed for success, or a poultry pie!

With needles that dance, I conquer each square,
A blanket of humor, in the cold winter air.
Each stitch tells a story, each knot's a new dare,
Threads of my journey, woven with flair.

In this tapestry, laughter's the thread,
With each silly stitch, my worries are shed.
So I'll knit with delight, till my fingers turn red,
It's a colorful canvas of joy overhead.

A Journey Encased in Metal

On a shiny chain, it sways so bright,
A jingle-jangle, what a sight!
It opens doors both near and far,
But mostly leads to the nearest bar!

With twists and turns, it's quite a ride,
Unlocking giggles we can't hide.
A treasure trove of sticky notes,
Of half-baked dreams and silly quotes.

They say it guards the secrets deep,
But really, just a place to keep
A stale gum and crumbs of cake,
And all my hopes of being great!

It's not for locks, it's more for laughs,
A shiny friend for all my gaffes.
So take a swing, give it a turn,
Let's unlock joy, it's our concern!

Secrets Close to Heart.

Tucked away, a mystery rides,
Bouncing gently, it never hides.
It whispers truths with a cheeky grin,
Of all the mischief we could begin!

In midnight talks and silly flings,
It guards my hopes like secret kings.
A flip, a twist, what will it show?
Perhaps my crush or socks with a toe!

Oh what a charm, what playful jest,
It holds my laughter, it knows me best.
So let it dangle, let it sway,
It makes me smile every day!

It's not just metal, it's a good friend,
With quirky tales that never end.
Together we unlock the fun,
Under the moon, we dance and run!

Unlocking Dreams

A little pendant, big on glee,
It could unlock a crazy spree!
With hopes and wishes nested tight,
It's a ticket to delight!

Shimmering bright, it swings and spins,
Could open doors or just my sins.
Lost in daydreams, what might I find?
A corn dog or a cat that's blind!

Dreams of travel, oh what a scheme,
Each jingly jangle fuels the dream.
Let's toss our fears into the sea,
And laugh away, just you and me!

So here it hangs, a charming muse,
Turning dull days into blues.
Unlocking giggles and plans anew,
Who knew a trinket could feel so true?

Pendant of Secrets

We wear our laughter, bright and bold,
With little secrets quietly told.
A charm that dangles, full of fun,
Ready to shine in the morning sun!

It holds my dreams like candy stashed,
With every jump and every splash.
A bit of mischief is what it brings,
And wild adventures like errant kings!

With whispers shared in playful tones,
And all my thoughts in silly phones.
It jangles lightly with every sway,
Leading me toward a wackier day!

So take a peek, come join the ride,
Around my neck is joy, I confide.
In this journey, we'll laugh and play,
With secrets wrapped in humor's sway!

Symphonies of Unlocked Spaces

In pockets deep, a touch of sound,
A jingle that twirls all around.
With every step, a tune to play,
Unlocking laughter along the way.

In cupboard doors that squeak and squeal,
Past the old cat, affection's zeal.
Each turn reveals a new charade,
In the dance of keys, we all parade.

So join the waltz, let giggles spark,
As corners hide a joke or quark.
With jingling friends, let joy ignite,
We'll sing our way from day to night.

A symphony of jests and glee,
Where every lock's a mystery.
Let's laugh and play, the world to tease,
For every key unlocks with ease.

Talismans of Time's Tapestry

In a twist of fate, oh what a sight,
Time's fabric frays in morning light.
A jester's grin, a wink of fun,
These charms unite, and mysteries run.

With each small jangle, stories grow,
Like vines that dance in a quirky show.
They hide in shadows, curl in light,
Unlocking treasures deep in night.

Tick-tock, the clock starts to hum,
As secrets weave, let laughter come.
We spin the tales, we spin the thread,
With every giggle, the past is bred.

A tapestry bright, woven with cheer,
In moments lost, we hold them dear.
So join the fun, unlock your fate,
For every tick, there's love to create.

Accessory of the Soul's Quest

An odd little charm, with curious grace,
It dangles low, adds flair to space.
With whims and giggles, it shakes and sways,
In its silly dance, our hearts it plays.

What doors shall open with a jig?
Each twist and turn feels rather big.
A knick-knack here, a doorknob there,
Unlocking laughter, oh what a flair!

The quest for joy, we embark anew,
With mischievous trinkets, always a few.
They wriggle and giggle, such playful things,
Unlocking the joy that a good joke brings.

It's not just an accessory, we proclaim,
But a token of fun, and never of shame.
With every chuckle, every light jest,
We find ourselves on a merry quest.

Guardian of Unspoken Lengths

In the depths of pockets, secrets dwell,
With giggly guards, they know them well.
Each silent key, a watchful friend,
Holding giggles that never end.

Through creaky doors and whispers low,
They guide our steps, where laughter flows.
With a nudge and wink, they brightly gleam,
Unlocking fun, a whimsical dream.

For in the night, with stars aglow,
Each laugh a twinkle, each jest a show.
These little keepers, with cheeky grace,
Guard the tales of our silly race.

So let's lift the veil, and let it flow,
For every key knows what we don't show.
In playful whispers, they keep the score,
A guardian's giggle, forevermore.

Charm of Serendipity

I found a trinket on my walk,
A jingle that made my dog squawk.
It turned out to be my lost old shoe,
Who knew it brought such joy to you?

A squirrel thought it was a nut,
And tried to take it, just my luck!
I chased him down, but oh, so slow,
He laughed and left, the thief in tow.

Now every step's a dance, you see,
With jingles and jangles, just me and me.
Life's little surprises, they never get old,
Just like that shoe that barely turned gold.

So keep your eyes wide and your heart light,
For treasures appear in the oddest sight.
With each twist and turn, oh what a ride,
In this charm of life, we'll always confide.

Emblem of Hidden Courage

In pockets deep, I found a toy,
A smiling face, it filled with joy.
A hidden medal, oh what a find,
It says 'Brave Knucklehead'—too true, combined.

A story untold, a dance quite bold,
With friends around, we laugh 'til old.
From clanging pots to silly hats,
Courage blooms in the quirkiest chats.

We marched to the beat of invisible drums,
With animated moves, we played the clums.
Each slip, each trip, a badge of pride,
In this emblem of courage, we all coincide.

So raise a cup to the brave and odd,
Who finds the fun in each time they trod.
Life's wild glory, embrace every chance,
With laughter and quirks, let's dance, let's dance!

Keyring of Daring Journeys

My adventure's keyring has grown so vast,
With odd souvenirs and stories amassed.
From a bottle cap to a tiny frog,
Each trinket holds tales under the fog.

A rubber band and a twisty straw,
My backpack's bursting, it's quite the jaw.
Collecting oddities, oh what a spree,
Setting out on journeys, just my friends and me.

We dodged puddles and ran from the sun,
Through wild fields where we laughed and spun.
Emblems of daring, oh how they sing,
In this journey of laughter, we find every swing.

With a jangle and jive, we'll chart new seas,
Each curious find like a soft summer breeze.
So hold on tight to your whimsical crew,
In the keyring of life, there's always something new.

Necklace of Timeless Wonders

A string of beads and colors bright,
Each one a wink of sheer delight.
In my laughter hang tales of old,
As funny as goblins who never grow bold.

I swirl and twirl in my shiny threads,
Chasing echoes of the mustered reds.
Every bead a laugh, a giggle, a slip,
With a pinch of grace, do a little flip.

We dance through the market, full of cheer,
As my necklace jingles, all draw near.
Tales told in colors that sparkle and shine,
In this charming chaos, joy intertwines.

So wear your quirks like a badge of grace,
With time as your partner, embrace the space.
In a life made of wonders, let's join the fun,
For laughter and stories can never be done.

Charm of Elemental Echoes

In a world where echoes dance,
I wear this charm, it takes a chance.
With every step, a laugh, a jig,
The neighbors think I've lost a big!

Wind whispers secrets, oh so sly,
It tickles my ears, I can't deny.
I trip on clouds, float on a breeze,
Still searching for my missing keys!

Fire flickers with a cheeky smile,
It warms my heart, ignites my style.
I juggle embers in a hat,
And wonder where my socks went at!

Water splashes, making me grin,
I dance in puddles, let the fun begin.
Earth rolls its eyes, what a sight to see,
As I giggle and trip over a tree!

The charm around my neck's quite sly,
It leads me to laughter as I fly.
With elemental echoes all around,
I'm the silliest jester to be found!

Atlas of Forgotten Realms

A map all wrinkled with stories untold,
Each line a giggle, each fold pure gold.
I venture forth to find lost lands,
Where jellybeans grow from candy sands.

Dragons dance in polka dots,
With silly hats and funny pots.
They sip on tea, then take a flight,
While I chase rainbows at half past night.

There's a kingdom ruled by cupcakes sweet,
Where frosting flows, and crows have feet.
Adventures galore in every nook,
I've even drawn a fish in a book!

I stumble upon a castle made of cheese,
And dine with mice on crackers and peas.
In realms forgotten, I find delight,
In this atlas, every map's a fright!

With secrets beneath my jester's hat,
I prance and laugh, and oh, imagine that!
Every page a giggle, a screech, a pout,
In my world of laughter, I dance about!

Touchstone of Infinite Possibilities

A pebble in my pocket, oh what a find,
With giggles and wiggles, it's one of a kind.
I toss it high, see where it lands,
In giggly realms with giggly bands.

It turns to a frog, then hops away,
In sunny meadows where unicorns play.
I chase my shadow, it's quite the tease,
The frog just croaks while I dance with ease.

A twirl, a whirl, I spin around,
The ground shakes with laughter, what a sound!
It's a touchstone of fun in every way,
With each hop and skip, I dare to play.

A fortune cookie holds dreams quite wild,
"Giggle at troubles, be a carefree child!"
I munch it down, then yell, "Ta-da!"
While clowns in bicycles zoom with a ha-ha!

Infinite paths before my eyes,
With each step, I'm more surprised.
A pebble, a touchstone, in my hand,
Leads me to these lands so grand!

Medallion of Memories

I wear a medallion with tales galore,
Each memory tickles as I explore.
A moment of laughter, a prank so sly,
It echoes back, oh my oh my!

I recall a day when socks went missing,
The cat just giggled, I swear, it'd be hissing.
What a chase, what a race,
Turned out they were just in his space!

A birthday bash where pies took flight,
I ducked just in time, that was quite the sight!
And grandma's wink when I told a joke,
Made everyone laugh till they nearly choked.

I twirl this medallion just for fun,
Each memory spins like a wild run.
It takes me back with a sideways glance,
To moments of joy, in a silly dance!

So here I am, with stories to share,
A medallion of memory, laughter in the air.
With every chuckle, I'm learning the clue,
That life is a jest, and love is the glue!

Secrets in Silver

In an old shoebox, I found a thing,
A shiny object that makes me sing.
Is it a key or just a spoon?
It could unlock magic or lead to doom!

I tried it on the fridge, gave it a turn,
And my leftovers danced, oh how they churn!
Next, to the closet, a jiggle and twist,
But all that emerged was an old sock mist!

A secret life of whirrs and clicks,
Unlocking laughter, oh what a fix!
Every turn brought a chuckle or sigh,
Is it a riddle or just a lie?

So now it's a charm on my silly chain,
Turning my day bright, never mundane.
Who knew a trinket could spark such fun?
In a world of wonders, I'm never done!

Enigma of Kismet

A shiny puzzle, hanging with glee,
What mysteries does it hold for me?
I waved it at my cat, she stared in fright,
Did I just unleash her feline plight?

I tossed it in the air, it bounced and rang,
But all I heard was a distant clang.
My cousin thought it was a lost car key,
But it opened up a world of glee!

A game of chance, a riddle for fools,
I laughed as it jiggled and played with the stools.
It beckons adventure in every swing,
Yet it's just a thing, with no worthy ring!

So here's to the trinkets that cause a stir,
Whispering secrets without a slur.
In the land of nonsense, it's purely divine,
A symbol of whimsy, forever mine!

Threads of Discovery

A silver charm with a quirky flair,
Tied up in laughter, floating in air.
Is it a button or something more strange?
With every twist, it seems to rearrange!

I followed it once, it led me to jest,
A tumble of socks, it knew where to rest.
Next, it revealed a curious plight,
My goldfish waltzing under moonlight!

I wear it with pride, though it's quite absurd,
It's a jester's crown, spreading the word.
A magical loop that never goes slack,
Full of surprises and a penchant to crack!

So here I declare, in laughter we trust,
For each little loop holds whimsical dust.
In the kingdom of giggles, we're all in a trance,
With threads of discovery, let's dance!

Pendant of Silent Whispers

A pendant of secrets, swinging with flair,
Collecting mischief, without a care.
Told my friends it unlocks a door,
But it only leads to an ice cream store!

With each little jingle, it starts a croon,
An empty cupboard escapes the gloom.
A bell for a cat, or toy for a pup,
With a wink it says, "Come on! Drink up!"

A whisper of giggles, it cracks me wide,
I'm convinced it's where all joy does hide.
Searching for trouble in every nook,
Turns out it's just a silly old book!

So here's to the charm, this pendant of catch,
Spinning tales with every little match.
In the world of giggles, I wear it with pride,
A piece of laughter, forever my guide!

Binding of Essential Truths

A twinkle on a chain so bright,
Hiding secrets day and night.
With every jingle, comes my fate,
Is it magic, or just my mate?

A pocket full of jumbled cues,
I wear it like an old pair of shoes.
It scoffs at my bewildered face,
A riddle wrapped in a strange embrace.

Can it unlock my lost remote?
Or open doors where dreams dote?
With every twist, my laughter flows,
This charm just teases, who really knows?

In meetings where I feign a grin,
This trinket keeps my thoughts within.
Each jingle, a tickle to my mind,
Oh, secret keeper, be so kind!

Unlocking the Unfamiliar

Around my neck, a shimmering prize,
It burbles secrets, what a surprise!
Each turn of the charm, a giggle escapes,
Is it wisdom or just quirky shapes?

A twist and a turn, a riddle awaits,
Unlocking the fruitcake of our fates.
Is this a key or just a joke?
Or simply a chat with a friendly bloke?

Oh, the mysteries of dinner plans,
This necklace knows my life's demands.
Will it conjure dessert or a foreign dish?
I ponder these thoughts and start to wish.

With every chime, awareness grows,
Life's a puzzle, who really knows?
Tangled in laughter, I wear my prize,
Unlocking joy through awkward tries!

Necklace of Infinite Journeys

A dangling bauble with tales untold,
Carved from laughter, it's worth its gold.
It jingles and jangles with every twist,
A passport to places with no chance missed.

From kitchens to couches, adventures begin,
It promises wonders tucked under my chin.
Each jolt and jive, a whimsy ride,
With this charm, I take a stride.

A trip to the moon or to Mars' red dust,
Always on time, in this I trust.
It whispers of journeys, funny and wild,
Oh, what tales it tells of a mischievous child!

So join me dear friend in giggles and grins,
With this necklace, the fun never thins.
Each clink a reminder of joy and their quirks,
Infinite journeys through timeless works.

Sigil of Solitude

Hanging close, a charm of peace,
Wrapped in wonder, my worries cease.
With every shift, a chuckle peeks,
It can't speak, but oh, it tweaks!

A hidden gem of odd design,
It pokes at dreams like cheap red wine.
In solitude, we share our quests,
Forgotten socks, or jesters in vests.

Oh, how I fumble with giggling grace,
My one true friend in this spacious place.
A confounding sigil of slow, sweet laughs,
Unlocking awkward like broken drafts.

So here I wear, a symbol true,
With laughter stemming from moments few.
In solitude's embrace, wit starts to flow,
This pendant of chuckles steals the show!

Chains of Memory

A jingle in my pocket, oh what could it be?
Perhaps a spare car key, or a lock for a tree.
My mind is a maze where old secrets are kept,
Each jangle a laugh, where my memories leapt.

I searched high and low, even under my bed,
For a clue to the mystery that danced in my head.
Was it a key to the kingdom of lost candy stash?
Or a remnant of moments that faded so fast?

In my kitchen drawer, they seem to align,
Spoons, forks, and paperclips, forming a line.
But the real treasure lies in the laughter they bring,
When I find silly magnets that start to sing.

So I wear them with pride, these chains of delight,
My old jingling buddies bring joy day and night.
Each clink and each clatter, a sweet serenade,
Of the funny, the quirky, the life that I made.

Charm of Revelation

A trinket or token, one that makes me grin,
Each time it pops out, wins a cheeky win.
A whispered reminder of days once so wild,
My secret world safe, like a forgetful child.

Now it swings with flair, like a dancer's fine twirl,
Surprises in my pocket, oh what a whirl!
A button, a charm, or perhaps a lost toy,
It brings out the giggles, the purest of joy.

Tangled in laughter, the stories entwined,
With each little throwback, I playfully find.
Like a game of hide-and-seek with my past,
Every strange little artifact, spells out a blast.

So I cherish these gems, each giggle and snort,
In the chaos of life, they provide a report.
With charm in abundance, I laugh through the fray,
Unraveling joy in the light of the day.

Treasure Beneath the Skin

Strange marks on my arms, each one tells a tale,
Of mishaps and laughter, like a curious whale.
A bruise from a fall, oh, what a fine gift!
With memories embedded, they give me a lift.

A smudge from my kitchen, a dash of bright hue,
Each splotch I like to flaunt, fresh stories anew.
Hidden beneath layers, treasures alive,
They spark little giggles that make me survive.

Like badges of honor for all that I've done,
The memories stitched in with a dash of some fun.
Yikes! What's that? A splatter from lunch?
And here's a wild adventure from an innocent munch.

So I show off my scars, my badges of joy,
Each mark is a chapter, and I'm no decoy.
With memories beneath, my skin's like a map,
Of all of life's laughs and an occasional mishap.

The Hinge of Hope

A door that swings wide with a creak and a laugh,
Each squeak is a friend, a jolly old gaffer.
What lies on the other side? A mystery grand,
A place filled with giggles and maybe some sand.

It's my little portal to silliness pure,
Where daydreams take flight, and joy's the encore.
With each turn of the knob, a chuckle is found,
As possibilities whirl like leaves on the ground.

In this hallway of humor, I dare to explore,
With every burst open, I'm richer than before.
A wardrobe of wonder, closet of cheer,
Where laughter takes shape, and fun draws near.

So I step through this opening, heart full in tow,
Embracing the magic, letting whimsy grow.
For in every hinge lies a spark that ignites,
The laughter of friendship and delightful sights.

Unlocking Secrets

In pockets deep, I found a thing,
A shiny charm that likes to cling.
It jangles loud when I must sneak,
Causing chaos every week.

My friends all laugh, they roll their eyes,
At my adventures filled with sighs.
I've locked a cat inside my room,
She plots revenge, her eyes in gloom.

A box of treasure, locked up tight,
But all I found was lots of fright.
The neighbors watched, they thought it neat,
As I found more escapes to meet.

With every twist, with every turn,
I learned that keys, they really burn.
Not for the doors, but all the fun,
When laughter sparkles in the sun.

Pendant of Possibilities

A pendant bright with secrets dressed,
It bounces 'round regardless of rest.
Each time I bend down to pick up crumbs,
I find my keys, and here comes hums!

On dates it dangles, causing glee,
I trip and fumble, 'Oh, look at me!'
Each lock I pass, it winks and shouts,
Unlock this world; no need for doubts!

The awkward moments, I can't deny,
A key for hearts, oh me, oh my!
For every slip on staircase grace,
The pendant leads to an odd embrace.

With laughter loud and silly grace,
I wear this charm, a wild chase.
Who knew a trinket held such cheer?
Spinning stories far and near!

Heartstrings and Hidden Doors

A heart-shaped charm beneath my shirt,
Leads me to adventures, what a flirt!
With every twist and jingle sound,
I find new friends, oh joy unbound!

In every corner, secrets bide,
A tiny door where dreams abide.
I peek inside, and what do I see?
A dance party hosted just for me!

My heartstrings tug, they pull and tease,
Unlocking joy with every breeze.
All the locks that hold me tight,
Are merely words of sheer delight!

I slip and slide through luck's own hatch,
With giggles loud and a heart to catch.
Behind each door, a laugh anew,
The world's my stage, and so are you!

Whispered Access

A whisper soft, I hear it clear,
Telling tales that bring good cheer.
With every step, I play this game,
Unlocking joy, it makes me lame!

In crowded rooms, the giggles flow,
As I unlock what they don't know.
With clumsy grace and smiles to share,
I unlock friendship, everywhere.

The tiny key, what fun it brings,
To open doors for silly things.
A toast to laughs, a wink from fate,
What's behind this door? Let's not wait!

I twirl around, a dancing spree,
With whispered secrets, come dance with me!
A key to laughter, light as air,
Unlocking joy beyond compare!

www.ingramcontent.com/pod-product-compliance
Lightning Source LLC
Chambersburg PA
CBHW070005300426
43661CB00141B/242